Scooter Gets the Point

Story by MOTHER MELANIA

Mother Melania is the abbess of Holy Assumption Monastery in Calistoga, CA. She has written several series of children's books, including The Twelve Great Feasts for Children, The Three-Day Pascha, Old Testament Stories for Children, and Fearless and Friends (a series of animal fables designed to teach children virtues in an engaging way). Her dog was named Scooter, but he was MUCH better behaved than this Scooter!

Illustration by ANTHONY CALLAS

A love for drawing and mathematics as a youth sprouted into a life long career as an architect and construction manager, Anthony also served in missions with the OCMC in Uganda, Mexico, and Albania. He lives in Colorado with his wife, three children, two dogs, and three cats and they all attend St Catherine Greek Orthodox Church in Greenwood Village, but leave the pets at home.

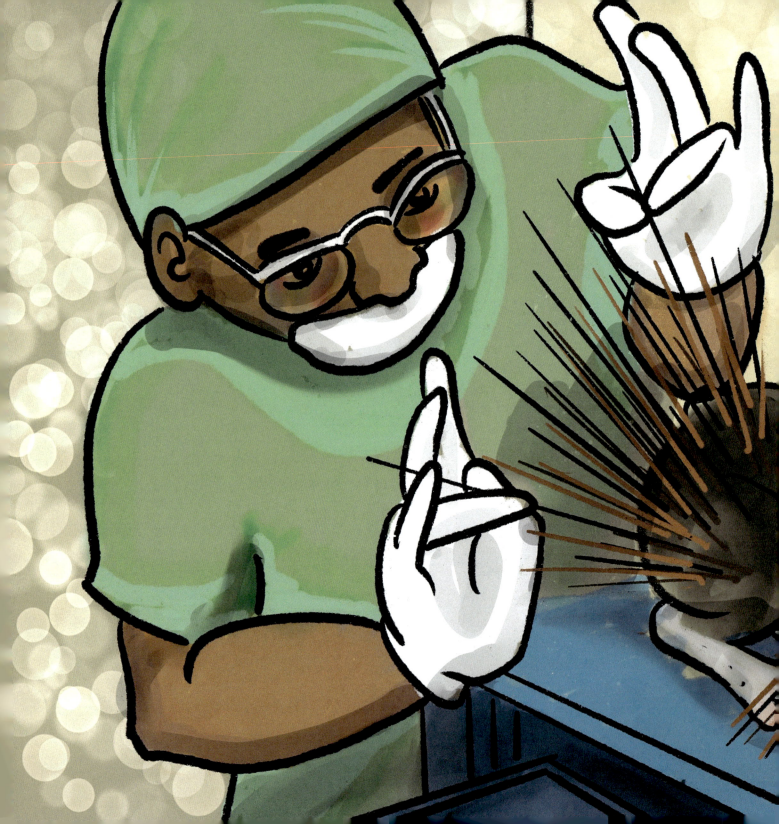

Scooter Gets the Point

Volume 1 in the Adventures of Kenny & Scooter

Text © copyright 2019 by Mother Melania
Illustrations © copyright 2019 by Anthony Callas

All rights reserved.

Published by Holy Assumption Monastery
1519 Washington St.
Calistoga, CA 94515
Phone: (707) 942-6244
Website: http:\\holyassumptionmonastery.com
Email: sisters@holyassumptionmonastery.com

ISBN: 978-1-946991-04-1

Made in the USA
Lexington, KY
24 November 2019